All th[...]

Betty Jacobs

CONTENTS

Bulb (Common) Onions

Botanical Name: *Allium cepa*, Cepa Group
Other Names: (Fr.) *oignon;* (Ger.) *Zwibel;* (It.) *cipolla;* (Sp.) *cebolla*
Life Span: Half-hardy perennial, usually grown as a long-season annual

How to Choose the Right Variety

The right variety is more important for onions than it is for most other vegetables. If you pick a variety adapted to the wrong part of the country (say, trying to grow the sweet Vidalia-type onions in the Northeast), you could end up with nice scallions but no bulbs. The formation of bulbs in different varieties is controlled by how the plants respond to day length. When daylight reaches the right number of hours for that variety, the onion plant stops putting out leaves and starts producing a bulb. The eventual size of the mature bulb depends on how much leaf growth the plant has produced at the time bulb formation starts. If the onion plant hasn't achieved enough top growth (either because it was planted too late or because the variety needs a different day length), the plants won't be

able to make bulbs. A cool start encourages the heavy leaf growth necessary for building up good-sized bulbs. Variety alone doesn't ensure good onions; you also need to provide fertile soil, so plants get the nutrients they need to produce good top growth.

Onions are grouped into short-day, long-day, and intermediate varieties. *Short-day onions* are adapted to growing in southern climates (south of 35° latitude), as they need only 11 or 12 hours of daylight to stimulate bulb formation. They also need mild winters (where temperatures don't go below about 20°F), as they're planted in late fall and grow through the winter. Bulb formation is triggered when days start to get longer in spring. The long winter growing season gives these varieties plenty of time to produce lots of leaves, so they can develop impressively large mature onions by late spring or early summer. The extra-sweet onion grown in Vidalia, Georgia ('Granex 33' or 'Yellow Granex') is a short-day variety.

Gardeners north of 35° latitude need to grow *long-day varieties.* (The 35° runs approximately through Flagstaff, Albuquerque, Memphis, and Charlotte.) These put out leaves during the long days of northern summers; they don't start making bulbs until the days start getting shorter (14 to 15 hours) as summer wanes.

Intermediate-day varieties, as you might expect, fall somewhere between the other two. They don't need the extra-long days of northern areas, but they need a long growing season. They can be planted from seeds sown outdoors in fall anywhere south or west of Zone 7 (below 35°N latitude and up the West Coast through the Pacific Northwest). Intermediate-day varieties can be grown in the North, but only if started from transplants rather than seeds or sets; otherwise, the growing season won't be long enough to form good bulbs.

There's usually a tradeoff between sweetness and storage quality in onion varieties. The onions with the sweetest flavor typically don't store as well as the more pungent types. Many of the largest and sweetest onions are short-day varieties. Many of the best keepers are long-day

Did You Know?

The onion is one of the oldest vegetables known. It belongs to a genus of about 280 species of bulbing plants, all having a very distinctive smell. There are hundreds of cultivated varieties, which vary in appearance, pungency, and keeping qualities. They are widely distributed over the Northern Hemisphere, mostly in regions with a temperate climate.

varieties; while these have a pungent flavor when raw, they lose their bite when cooked and also become milder in storage.

When choosing a variety, read the descriptions you'll find in seed catalogs. A catalog should tell you which varieties grow best in what areas, the number of days from planting to maturity, the shape and flavor of the bulb, and whether it is suitable for eating raw, cooking, pickling, and/or storing.

Seeds, Transplants, or Sets?

You can start your onions by sowing seeds, by buying started plants, or by planting sets. Starting onions from seeds gives you the widest choice of varieties (so be sure you choose one that's the right day length). It takes 100–120 days for most varieties to develop mature bulbs, so plan on starting seeds indoors where the growing season is shorter. You can, of course, use the immature onions as scallions (green onions) sooner. If stored in a cool, dry spot, onion seeds should remain viable for two years.

Buying plants gives you a small choice of varieties, but it enables you to produce an edible crop more quickly. While relatively expensive, it's a good choice if you live where the growing season is short and want to produce the largest onions. You can often find flats of seedlings at local garden centers, and now you can order pencil-thick transplants from many standard seed companies. Mail-order transplants are shipped at the appropriate planting time for your area; while they may arrive looking tired from their journey, they recover quickly if planted soon after arrival.

Planting sets gives you even less choice of varieties (unless you've grown your own the previous year; see page 8 for how to do so). But you'll get green onions very quickly, and the bulbs will mature three or more weeks before those grown from seeds. Sets are also available by mail order, for less expense than transplants. They're a good choice for short-season areas, or where onion diseases have been a problem (sets and transplants are more disease-resistant than are direct-seeded onions).

How to Grow Good Onions

Onions prefer a loose, crumbly, well-drained, fertile soil with a pH between 6.0 and 7.0. If you have any doubt about whether your soil

---

Some Recommended Varieties

Here are a few onion varieties for different areas of the United States. There are many more that are equally good. Check catalog descriptions or ask your local Cooperative Extension Service or garden center. Varieties sold as sets usually do well in most regions; they may be described only as "red," "white," or "yellow" sets.

Short-Day Varieties for the North

Plants: 'Yellow Sweet Spanish' (large and mild); 'Walla Walla Sweet' (large, white with yellow skin, one of the sweetest onions for the North); 'Red Burgermaster' (red-and-white flesh). *Note:* Transplants of intermediate-day varieties also grow well in the North.

Sets: 'Stuttgarter' (yellow, good for storage); 'Ebenezer'

Seeds: 'Early Yellow Globe' or 'New York Early' (early maturing, yellow); 'Yellow Sweet Spanish' (large bulbs); 'White Sweet Spanish'; 'Copra' (one of the best keepers); 'Southport Red Globe' (red skin, pink to white flesh); 'Mars' (relatively early, red)

Intermediate-Day Varieties for Middle Latitudes

Plants: 'Stockton Red' (good keeper; transplants do well in all regions)

Sets: 'Stuttgarter'; 'Ebenezer'

Seeds: 'Early Yellow Globe'; 'Candy' (white flesh, one of the sweetest, also grows well in the North); 'Red Torpedo' (mild, nonbolting, disease-resistant)

Short-Day Varieties for the South

Plants: 'Yellow Granex' or 'Granex 33' (very sweet, type grown in Vidalia, Ga.), 'White Bermuda' or 'Crystal Wax' (very sweet)

Sets: 'Ebenezer'

Seeds: 'Yellow Granex' or 'Granex 33' (very sweet, large); 'Texas Grano '1015Y' or 'Texas Supersweet' (very sweet, large, disease-resistant); 'White Bermuda' or 'Crystal Wax' (very sweet); 'Red Burgundy' or 'Red Hamburger' (sweet, red skin, red-and-white flesh); 'Yellow Bermuda' (white flesh, small necks)

---

is well drained, grow onions in raised beds, that is, 4 inches (10 cm) higher than the surrounding soil. Incorporate lots of organic matter to improve drainage and fertility. You can add organic matter at any time, but it's best to do this well before planting. That means the fall before planting, where onions will be planted or transplanted in spring; or a month or two before where onions will be planted in spring. Spread a couple of inches (about 5 cm) of compost or well-aged manure over the planting area and turn under with a garden fork or till in. If a soil test shows your soil is acidic, it's a good idea to add lime at the same time that you add organic matter; add only enough lime to raise the pH to the ideal range, as too much is worse than too little.

A week or so before planting or transplanting, spread a balanced fertilizer (such as 5-10-10) at the rate recommended on the fertilizer label for vegetables. Rake the soil to create a level planting surface.

Start Onion Seeds Indoors

Where the growing season is short, start onion seeds indoors 10 to 12 weeks before the last expected frost. Onion seeds will germinate in 7 to 10 days if kept between 64° and 77°F (16°–25°C). They'll germinate at a temperature as low as 45°F (8°C) but will take longer. Once they sprout, grow seedlings under fluorescent lights or in a greenhouse or cold frame.

1. Fill a seed flat with sterile potting soil, and tap it down gently.
2. Shake seeds thinly over the soil, so that they're well spaced.
3. Cover seeds with no more than ¼ inch of fine soil. If some seeds show through the next day, sprinkle a little more soil over them, but never bury them deeply.
4. Stand the whole flat in a tray of water, so that the water comes only about three-quarters of the way up the sides of the flat. The water will be drawn up into the soil. Remove the flat from the water as soon as the soil surface looks damp. Let the surplus water drain out of the flat. Keep in a warm spot to speed germination.

Starting Onions from Seeds

To give the onions the longest possible growing season, seeds should be sown outdoors in fall where winters aren't too severe (Zones 7 and warmer). In Zone 7, sow onion seeds (intermediate-day or short-day varieties) from late August to mid September; in the warmer parts of Zone 8 and Zone 9, sow in October (short-day varieties). In colder zones where the growing season is long enough (100 to 120 days; the actual length of time needed depends on the variety), you can sow seeds outside in early spring. Plant seeds a month before the final spring frost, when the soil has warmed to at least 45°F (about 7°C). In areas with shorter seasons, start seeds indoors.

5. As soon as the onions start to show, move to a bright spot such as under fluorescent lights. Once they've sprouted, they don't need as much warmth.
6. Keep seedlings moist by bottom watering when they begin to look dry. Once the little plants are well up, you can water them with a fine spray from above. Thin to four seedlings per inch, or three plants to each 1- or 2-inch-diameter cell.
7. When the onions are about as thick as a pencil, they should be hardened off. Put the flat outside for longer and longer periods for a few days, starting with the warmest time of day, and eventually leave them out all night. This hardening off should take about two weeks.
8. To make the seedlings easier to transplant, lift them and wash the soil off the roots, trim any extra-long roots, and trim the green leaves to about 5 inches (10 cm) long.

Bottom watering keeps seedlings moist.

Allow ½ ounce (14 g) of seeds for every 100 feet (30 m) of row. Plant seeds ½ inch apart in rows, spacing rows 12 to 18 inches apart. Cover seeds with ¼ to ½ inch of soil.

Many gardeners thin their rows twice, the first time when the seedlings are very small and the next time when the plants are large enough to be enjoyed as scallions. Thin young seedlings to 2 inches apart, then harvest scallions as needed to leave mature plants 4 inches apart to form bulbs. (Final spacing should be 6 inches for large varieties.)

Starting Onions from Sets

Sets are small, dry onion bulbs that were grown the previous year but not allowed to mature. They produce the earliest onions; they're also a good choice if you want to grow large onions where the growing season is short. A pound of sets will plant about 50 feet of row (0.5 kg for 15 m). Sets can be planted outdoors four to six weeks before the last expected frost. Press sets into the soil so the

---

Grow Your Own Sets from Seeds

By planting seeds too late (about mid May), you can ensure that they won't have time to mature and will form only very small bulbs, or sets. When replanted the following spring, these tiny bulbs can finish developing; because they get a head start on the season, they'll form good-sized bulbs in much less time as soon as they get the right day-length signal.

Choose a sunny area of well-worked, weed-free soil. Sow the seeds thickly and don't thin the seedlings; this will help to keep bulbs small. Don't fertilize the seedlings; you don't want to encourage too much top growth or you'll end up with bulbs that are too large. (Overly large sets may bolt to seed the following spring.) Water as required. Lift them in late summer or as soon as the tops are dry. The bulbs, which should be under ¾ inch (approximately 2 cm) in diameter, will form no flower buds in cool storage. The following year, the bulbs will quickly produce edible "green" onions or, if left in the ground until late summer, will grow into good-sized bulb onions.

---

stem ends point up and they're not more than 1 inch (2.5 cm) below the surface, and 4 to 6 inches apart. Or plant the sets more closely (2 inches apart) and harvest the thinnings as scallions, eventually leaving 4 to 6 (10–15 cm) inches between plants. In this case you'll need about twice as many sets for the same amount of row (2 pounds for 50 feet; 1 kg for 15 m).

Transplanting Onions

Whether you've raised your own seedlings or bought plants, onions can be transplanted out about a month before the last frost date (they can handle temperatures as cold as 20°F, about -7°C). If you've grown your own, be sure to harden them off first. Mail-order transplants will arrive already hardened off.

Transplants should be set out about 1 inch deep (or at about the same level they were growing). Space standard varieties 4 inches apart, larger varieties 6 inches apart. If you plan to eat a lot of scallions, space transplants 2 to 3 inches apart and thin every other one to leave a final spacing of 4 to 6 inches (10–15 cm). If you prefer to plant in standard rows, space rows 12 to 18 inches apart. Onions also grow well in wide rows, which allow you to grow more plants in a smaller garden.

In wide rows, onions are spaced 4 to 6 inches (10–15 cm) apart in all directions in 4-foot-wide (1.2 m) beds. This method works well in raised beds. Two great advantages of this method are that you never have to walk on the beds — as anyone kneeling down can reach halfway across a 4-foot (1.2 m) bed to weed and cultivate — and no space is wasted between rows. Make your wide rows as many feet long as necessary to give you space to grow the quantity of onions you require.

Here's an example of how to calculate how many plants you'll need for wide-row planting. Assume a spacing of 5 inches (12.5 cm) between onions, with 4 inches (10 cm) from the edge of the bed to the first onion and 4 inches (10 cm) to the back edge of the bed, and you'll end up with eight onions per row. Every 5 inches (12.5 cm) along the bed will give you another row of eight onions, so a bed 5 feet (1.5 m) long will give you room for 12 rows. A wide bed 4 feet x 5 feet (1.2 x 1.5 m) therefore provides space for 8 x 12 = 96 onions. If you like to eat a lot of scallions, you can fit in even more onions by spacing plants 2½ inches (6.25 cm) apart in at least a few of the rows and gradually thinning alternate plants as scallions or small onions.

Care During Growth

Whichever way your onions are started, they'll all need the same care. Keep them free of weeds. Onions tolerate far less crowding from weeds than can many other vegetables. Because onion roots grow close to the surface, keep cultivation shallow. At no time while they're growing should soil be drawn up around the plants. Onions do better growing on or near the surface. For the largest onions, pull away the soil from the upper two-thirds of the bulb.

After plants have been growing for a month or so, they'll appreciate side-dressing with fertilizer, or a foliar feeding with liquid seaweed or fish emulsion; repeat in another month. Avoid giving onions too much nitrogen; you want to encourage good growth, but too much nitrogen will give you more leaves than bulb. Stop feeding plants about a month before harvest, or as soon as the necks start feeling soft.

If any of your onions send up a flower stalk, pull them up and eat them. Bulb onions that have started to bolt won't store well, so it's best to eat them before the flower stalk gets very big.

Onions need even moisture to grow well. A thin layer of mulch (1 to 2 inches of fine compost or chopped leaves) helps keep the soil moist and reduces weeds, but pull the mulch away from plant bases once bulbs begin forming. Water plants regularly until the tops start to yellow, then withhold water to help skins ripen for better storage. When the leaves have turned yellow and about a quarter have fallen over, bend tops over to direct energy from the leaves into the maturing bulbs. The back of a garden rake is handy for this job.

How to Harvest Onions

Once the tops have been bent over, it will take a few days (depending on the weather) for the leaves to dry enough to harvest your onions. When the tops are quite dry, lift the bulbs and leave them in the sun to dry, long enough so that any dirt on their roots is dry. To prepare for storage, you can braid the long dry tops and hang the braids. Or just cut off the tops, leaving 1 inch (2.5 cm) of stem on each bulb, and trim back the roots. Place trimmed onions in slatted crates, net bags, or old nylon stockings (tie a knot between each onion, and cut the stocking when you want to use an onion). Cure onions for several weeks by keeping them in a shed or under cover where air can circulate freely. While the weather is still dry and before frost is expected, move the onions into a dry, cool, frost-free, and (preferably) dark storage place.

Sweet, Vidalia-type Onions

There are a few tricks to growing the large, sweet onions called 'Vidalia' after the place in Georgia that made them famous. Their sweetness is a combination of the right variety, an exceptionally long growing season, and fertile soils low in sulfur. The largest, sweetest onions can be grown only in the South and in mild areas of the West because they're short-day varieties that are planted in fall and grown through the winter. They need winters that don't get below 20°F (7°C). If planted in early spring, these varieties will still produce good onions, but the bulbs won't be as large or as sweet as those grown through the winter.

The best varieties for sweet onions are 'Yellow Granex' or 'Granex 33' (the type grown in Vidalia, Georgia), 'Texas Grano '1015Y' or 'Texas Supersweet' (any variety with "Grano" in the name), and improved Bermuda types such as 'Excel'. In parts of the Northwest with winters mild enough for fall planting, the intermediate-day variety 'Walla Walla Sweet' produces large, very sweet onions. A new intermediate-day variety, 'Candy', also produces very sweet onions from spring planting in most parts of the country.

If onions are stressed by low fertility or lack of water while they're growing, their flavor will be more pungent, so it's important to keep plants well fed and watered. Sulfur also increases pungency; one secret to the sweetness of onions grown in Vidalia is the low sulfur content of the soils there. While you can't change the sulfur content of your soil, you can avoid increasing it by steering clear of fertilizers that contain sulfur (such as ammonium sulfate). Stop fertilizing about 30 days before you expect to harvest in order to keep onions as sweet as possible.

When the necks are well contracted and the skins are brittle, curing is complete. The ideal storage conditions for onions are quite cool, 36°F (2°C), and fairly dry, 60 to 70 percent relative humidity. Storage temperatures must not get above 45°F (7°C).

Use thick-necked onions first; they're not as good keepers as thin-necked bulbs. In general, sweet varieties don't store as well as (because they have a higher water content), so eat them first. Pungent varieties last the longest and often become sweeter in storage.

Braiding Onions

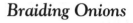

1. *Loop string around onion top.* 2. *Braid in second onion as shown.* 3. *Repeat with third onion and others.*

Scallions (Green Onions) and Pickling Onions

As already mentioned, the thinnings of immature bulb onions make good scallions. If you want just scallions, you can also plant varieties developed to form no bulbs, or only small ones. The bestknown variety of bulb onion grown specifically for scallions is 'White Lisbon'. It's easy to grow from seeds and is grown the same way as onions for bulbs. In climates with mild winters, a fall as well as a spring sowing is recommended so scallions can be harvested almost year-round. In hot climates, fall sowing is mandatory.

There are also a number of varieties of bunching onions such as 'Evergreen White' and 'Evergreen Hardy White' that produce long, thin, nonbulbing stems. These make good scallions that will stand over the winter months. (See Welsh onions on page 26.)

Pickling onions should have small bulbs, so they don't need a rich soil. You can also grow them spaced closely together to help keep bulbs small; thin seedlings to no more than 2 inches apart.

Chives

Botanical Name: *Allium schoenoprasum*
Other Names: (Fr.) *ciboulette;* (Ger.) *Schnittlauch;* (It.) *cpollina;* (Sp.) *cebolleta, cebollino*
Life Span: Hardy perennial (Zones 3–9); grow as a winter annual in hot climates
Appearance: Fine, dark green hollow leaves grow to a height of 8 to 12 inches (20–30 cm). Attractive flower heads like purple pom-poms appear at the end of tough stalks in late spring and summer. If they're not removed, hard black seeds will form inside each tiny flower (giving you volunteers near the parent plant), and the production of the edible leaves will fall off. The base of each leaf stem is like a miniature green onion; the roots are fine, white, and very free-growing.
Propagation: Chive plants are easy to find in any garden center, and sometimes even at the grocery store. If you want to grow your own, sow seeds indoors in early spring. Keep at a temperature of 60° to 80°F (15°–26°C) until they sprout. When they've germinated, seedlings should be moved to a cooler location under grow lights or in a cold frame. When seedlings are a few inches high, lift them from the soil, trim any extra-long roots, bunch together 10 or 12, and plant the bunches 8 inches (20 cm) apart. If you want to grow them in a pot, plant one bunch to a 4-inch pot.

Chives may also be propagated by dividing two, three, or four-year-old plants. Dig up the whole plant, shake or wash off the soil, and trim extra-long roots if desired. Divide the clump into several smaller clumps, each containing 8 or 10 bulblets. Replant 8 inches (20 cm) apart. A 5-inch (or larger) pot will be needed to grow these divided plants.

Cultural Requirements: Chives like moderately rich, well-worked soil. You may find it easiest to grow them in a separate area (such as an herb garden), or at least at the edge of the vegetable bed, so you won't have to work around them when tilling the soil for your vegetables. As they're likely to be in the same place for several years, prepare the bed thoroughly before planting. Spread an inch or so of compost over the area and atop this sprinkle dried steer manure (or standard fertilizer at rates recommended on label). Once a year, top-dress plants with compost or manure to keep them growing well; compost doubles as a good mulch to keep soil from splashing onto leaves.

Harvesting, Drying, Freezing, & Storing: Chives can be harvested when the green leaves are as short as 2 inches (5 cm) in early spring, though it's advisable to let them grow a little longer. Always cut about an inch above the white stems; don't harvest by snipping off the tips or plants will soon be covered with ugly brown cut ends. Keep cutting regularly all through the growing season, or the leaves will toughen.

Cut dry and held in an airtight plastic bag, chives will keep well in a refrigerator for three weeks or more. To freeze for cooking, use scissors to snip chives onto a cookie sheet that will fit into your freezer; leave in the freezer overnight. Then shake the frozen pieces into a zip-top plastic bag; store in the freezer and use as needed. Chives lose much of their flavor when dried and are useless for salads when they've been frozen. To provide a supply of fresh leaves for winter, grow chives indoors in 5-inch pots under fluorescent lights.

Quantity to Grow: If you're buying plants, start with two 4-inch pots to have enough to use the first year. In two years you can divide them to make about eight plants. Growing from seeds is more work and results are slower, but it's cheaper.

How to Use in the Kitchen: The whole plant has a delicate onion flavor. Chives can be snipped raw in vegetable salads, omelets, and many egg dishes; sprinkled in soup; made into chive butter for steaks and hamburgers; and used in cheese dishes or with all kinds of potatoes. They're also used in sauces such as remoulade and ravigote and are an absolute must for garnishing vichyssoise. Chive flowers are also edible and can be sprinkled over salads or used as a garnish.

Garlic

Botanical Name: *Allium sativum*
Other Names: Poor man's treacle; (Fr.) *ail*; (Ger.) *Knoblauch*; (It.) *aglio*; (Sp.) *ajo*
Life Span: Hardy perennial, though often treated as an annual
Appearance: Garlic leaves are 1 to 2 feet tall, narrow, and flat, emerging from a bulb formed of several small cloves held together by a papery skin. The flower clusters are white and enclosed in a sheath, which sometimes also contains tiny cloves or bulbils; they top a tough stalk some 24 inches (60 cm) high.
Propagation: Garlic is grown from individual cloves; it is seldom propagated by seed. Remove the papery skin covering the compound bulbs and break into individual cloves. Large cloves grow into large bulbs, so discard (or eat) the long slender cloves found in the heart of the bulb. Individual cloves should be planted 4 to 6 inches (10–12 cm) apart and 1 inch (2.5 cm) deep, slightly deeper — 2 to 4 inches — for fall planting in the North. Firm soil gently around cloves after planting. Though some prefer to plant in spring (as early as soil can be worked), most people plant in fall and most suppliers ship only in fall. Garlic will survive cold winters if planted around the time of the first expected frost and mulched well. Spring planting produces smaller cloves. Garlic will grow well in a sunny window box, but results from planting in pots (one clove to each 5-inch pot) aren't very satisfactory.

> ## ? Did You Know?
>
> The smell of garlic, both on the breath and on the hands, often discourages people from using it. Chewing a few leaves of fresh parsley or celery will usually deodorize your breath. To get the smell off your fingers, rub a little table salt on them and rinse in cold water.

Cultural Requirements: Garlic grows well in fertile, moist, well-drained soil. While neutral to slightly acidic soil is best, garlic will tolerate a pH between 5.5 and 8.0. Soil prepared for onions is satisfactory. Garlic needs full sun for good-quality bulbs. Provide a little fertilizer once spring growth begins; stop fertilizing as soon as plants start developing bulbs. Keep down the weeds. To allow the maximum development of the bulbs, pick off any flower heads that appear and keep the soil loose and friable. Proper watering is important. If the developing bulbs suffer drought, their growth will be checked; then when irrigated the newly developing cloves will sprout. If watered excessively, bulb quality and keeping quality will be impaired. So it's important to keep a balance between excessive moisture and excessively dry conditions. As with onions, all water should be withheld when the tops start to dry and bulbs begin to ripen.

Harvesting, Drying, Freezing, & Storing: Harvest as soon as the tops of the stalks turn brown (there's no need to bend over the tops of the plants as you would with onions). Otherwise, garlic should be harvested, dried, and stored in the same way as onions.

Garlic may be peeled, chopped, and frozen, but it's difficult to keep the smell in the packet and out of the freezer. Although dehydrated garlic powders are available commercially, the flavor is inferior to fresh garlic (it's also possible to dry your own; small chunks are easier to produce than garlic powder). Don't harvest the green tops; your cloves will suffer if you do. Grow garlic chives if you want garlic-flavored greens for salads and omelets.

Quantity to Grow: Assuming approximately 40 to 50 cloves per pound, you'll need 3 to 4 pounds of cloves to plant 50 feet of row (about 2 kg for 15 m) if you space cloves 4 inches apart. You can

---

Elephant Garlic

This garlic is a different species (*A. scorodoprasum*) that's less pungent than ordinary garlic. Its huge cloves are very mild in flavor, and much larger quantities can be used in cooking. It can be grown in a wide variety of climates; it will tolerate damper zones and somewhat less sunshine and warmth. It's grown the same way as ordinary garlic, though cloves should be planted at least 6 inches (15 cm) apart. You can plant as late as May, though fall planting is recommended, as for ordinary garlic.

expect to harvest 12 to 25 pounds (5–13 kg) from one 50-foot row, depending on the variety and growing conditions.

How to Use in the Kitchen: Garlic's flavor is distinctively pungent, and to some people objectionable, but it's probably the most important flavoring discovery — after onions — ever made, and it's used all over the world. Countless dishes can be improved by the addition of a little garlic.

To peel garlic and leave the cloves whole, put the concave side of the clove down on a firm (and washable) surface and press it gently with your thumb. The paperlike cover will split and come away, leaving the flesh ready to chop. If you want to crush and peel a clove at the same time, hold down the tip of a large kitchen knife placed flat on a chopping board, put the clove under the widest part, and hit it firmly with the flat of your hand; the clove will be nicely crushed and the skin will come away from it.

Garlic Varieties

When shopping for garlic to plant, you'll find two general types of varieties: soft-neck and hard-neck. Soft-neck garlic is the kind you find in the supermarket. These varieties have many small cloves in each bulb and, as you might expect from the name, a soft central stem. They have a long shelf life and don't generally produce flowers. Some soft-neck varieties of garlic include 'Italian', 'Polish White' (also known as 'New York White') and 'Gilroy California Late Garlic'.

Hard-neck types are varieties of rocambole (*A. sativum* var. *ophioscorodon*) bred for bigger bulbs. Hard-neck varieties produce bulbs with fewer but larger cloves around a woody central stalk. They're generally hardier than soft-neck varieties, with good flavor, but cloves may not last as long in storage as they tend to sprout sooner. Hard-neck or rocambole types produce a flowering stem in late spring; if left on the plant, the stem may grow around in a complete circle and produce small topsets at the end. (Serpent garlic, an old name for rocambole, comes from the stem's resemblance to a long neck with a pointed head at the end.) Remove all flower stems to redirect the plant's energy into bulb formation. 'German Red' is a common hard-neck variety; 'Spanish Roja' is another.

Garlic Chives

Botanical Name: *Allium tuberosum*
Other Names: Chinese chives, Oriental chives
Life Span: Hardy perennial (Zones 4–9). Garlic chives withstand frost but aren't as hardy as ordinary chives; in climates with long, severe winters, they may winter-kill unless given some protection.
Appearance: The dark green leaves grow about 12 inches (30 cm) long. They aren't hollow like ordinary chives; they look flat but are actually triangular in cross section. In late summer, clumps produce attractive clusters of starry white flowers on stalks above the leaves; the flowers have a surprisingly sweet fragrance.
Propagation: Plants of garlic chives aren't as widely available as ordinary chives, but you can find them anyplace that sells a good variety of herbs. Seeds should be started indoors in early spring, if you want to have leaves ready for use the first year; they sprout best at a temperature of 70° to 80°F (20°–26°C). When the tiny grasslike seedlings are large enough to handle, lift them gently from the soil, trim any extra-long roots, bunch together 10 or 12, and plant 10 inches apart. Three- or four-year-old plants may be divided in spring; in climates with mild winters dividing may also be done in the fall. Dig up the whole plant, wash soil off roots, and trim any extra-long roots. The little bulblets can then be separated easily. Bunch together six or eight and replant 10 inches (25 cm) apart.
Cultural Requirements: Garlic chives grow well in average soil. As with ordinary chives, you may find it easiest to grow them at the edge of the vegetable bed or in a separate area (such as an herb garden) so you won't have to work around them when tilling the vegetable bed. Before planting, enrich the soil with compost or aged manure (or dehydrated manure, available in bags at garden centers). In cooler climates, a well-drained, sheltered, sunny position is needed, such as near the south wall of a house. In hot, dry climates some summer shade is best. Remove flower stems and flower heads as soon as they fade and before they set seeds (otherwise, you'll find many volunteers popping up). To grow garlic chives indoors, use a 4-inch square pot or a 5-inch round one; when the plants have grown so the roots fill the pots, divide plants and repot into two or more pots. Garlic chives may also be grown in a sunny window box, but they need to be dug up and divided every year.

Harvesting, Drying, Freezing, & Storing: With a sharp knife or scissors, cut the garlic chive green about ½ inch (approximately 1 cm) above ground level. Do this to stimulate growth whether you need many or few leaves.

Quantity to Grow: Start with two plants, and divide them after the second year's growth. This should give you about eight new plants. If you start them from seeds, about a half-ounce (14 g) should give you more than enough plants the first summer.

How to Use in the Kitchen: Garlic chives can be used in place of ordinary chives when a delicate garlic flavor is called for. Until you are familiar with them, though, use sparingly.

Leeks

Botanical Name: *Allium porrum*
Life Span: Hardy biennial
Appearance: Leeks look like oversized scallions, but their leaves are flat, solid, and wrap almost all the way around the lower part of the plant. Leeks don't produce bulbs and are cultivated mainly for the use of the blanched lower leaves, which form a long cylindrical structure. This may be from 6 to 10 inches (15–20 cm) long and up to 2 inches (5 cm) in diameter, depending on the variety being grown. The flower heads and seeds, which don't usually appear until the second year, are typically onionlike in appearance.
Propagation: Leeks are usually grown from seeds, which remain viable for at least two years. (An uncommon type, a perpetual leek, produces side growths that can be planted out to produce another crop the following year.) At a temperature of 40°F (5°C), seeds take about 14 days to germinate. Leeks are a slow-growing crop (they take 70–110 days to reach maturity), so start them early, either indoors under lights or in a cold frame. For a late-fall or early-winter crop, sow 8 to 10 weeks before the last spring frost is expected; seedlings will be ready to transplant into the garden in 10 weeks. In warmer climates, leeks can be sown outdoors in fall under a floating row cover (to keep the soil cooler), grown through the winter, and harvested in spring or early summer before hot temperatures arrive. If you don't want to grow your own from seeds, leek transplants can be purchased at many garden centers (or see suppliers).
Cultural Requirements: Leeks thrive in a temperate or cool-temperate climate, in rich neutral to alkaline soil (pH 6.8–8.0). Prepare your ground as you would for onions, but add lime if needed to bring the pH into the correct range. A few days before transplant-

ing leeks outdoors, apply fertilizer to the planting area (follow recommended rates on label for vegetables) and mix or rake into the soil. When the leek seedlings are about 10 weeks old (about 8 inches or 20 cm tall), they're ready to plant into their permanent quarters. Space rows 1½ feet apart. Lift seedlings carefully from the pot or tray (you can trim any extra-long roots to make them easier to plant). Make holes 6 inches (15 cm) apart and about 6 inches (15 cm) deep. (A dibble — a planting tool that looks like a fat pointed stick — is handy here). Drop in a leek and fill each hole with water. This will wash down the soil to cover the roots. You don't want the soil packed tightly around the leek stems; as they grow they'll fill in the hole. You're aiming for a long, white (blanched) stem; by burying the plant like this you'll get it without all the trouble of growing leeks in trenches. To produce large leeks, side-dress with fertilizer or feed with liquid fish emulsion (or manure tea) once a month through the growing season. Flower stems don't usually appear until the spring following planting, but if they do, cut them off.

Harvesting, Drying, Freezing, & Storing: The first leeks should be ready a few weeks before the first frost. If you live in a climate where winters don't get below 10°F (-12°C), you can leave them in the ground and dig them as you need them. Where the ground freezes hard and deep, dig leeks as late as is practical and store them in a cool, frost-free place in sand — or clean them, slice, blanch, and store in the freezer. Leeks don't dry well.

Quantity to Grow: The first year allow about 20 leeks per person. The next year you can judge by your surplus or lack, and plant accordingly.

How to Use in the Kitchen: Leeks have a milder flavor than onions. In the United States, leeks are well known for their use in vichyssoise, and they give a distinctive flavor to many soups such as pot-au-feu and to fish stock. They are also delicious as a steamed or braised vegetable. They go well in lamb and egg dishes. When young, tender, and freshly dug, leeks can be eaten raw or sliced into long thin strips to garnish salads.

Potato Onions

Botanical Name: *Allium cepa*, Aggregatum Group
Other Names: Multiplier onion, underground onion
Life Span: Hardy perennial, often treated as an annual
Appearance: The stems, leaves, and roots of potato onions are similar to the common bulb onion, though the skins are copper colored and thicker. The bulbs are 1 to 2 inches in diameter and irregular in shape. Their flavor is typically onion. Each planted bulb (or offset) will produce a cluster of 8 to 10 bulbs of varying sizes at or just below the surface of the soil.

Propagation: Grow potato onions by replanting the smaller bulbs produced the year before; they seldom produce seeds. For an early summer crop, plant these bulbs in fall to midwinter in milder climates, or in very cold climates as soon as the soil can be worked in spring. Fall-planted bulbs reward you with the earliest green onions the following spring, so you may wish to try a couple and mulch them well even where winters are severe. Push the bulblets into the soil so that their tips are just buried, and leave 8 to 10 inches (20–25 cm) between each one. It isn't practical to grow these onions in pots or window boxes.

Cultural Requirements: Potato onions require the same type of soil and growing conditions as the common onion. Once bulbs have rooted, they shouldn't be transplanted. Weed by hand — the new offsets develop just below the surface of the soil and it's very easy to damage them, so don't use a hoe. Don't mulch, as this may slow their growth and ripening and, in a wet year, may keep soil too moist and cause bulbs to rot. When the clusters have worked to the surface, gently brush back the soil so bulbs are exposed to the sun. This will assist them to ripen. Don't expose the roots at this time.

Harvesting: Potato onions are often fully mature by midsummer. Harvest when the tops turn brownish yellow and treat them in the same way as you would the common bulb onion.

Quantity to Grow: Basing your calculations on a yield of 8 to 10 bulbs for every one planted, estimate the quantity you wish to use and store, including some to save to plant next year. It's difficult to estimate what weight of crop you can expect, as this will vary with climate, soil conditions, and your skill. Keep a record of production the first year to guide you in the future.

How to Use in the Kitchen: The mild-flavored potato onion can be used in any dishes in which you would use the common bulb onion.

Shallots

Botanical Name: *Allium cepa*, Aggregatum Group
Other Names: (Fr.) *échalote*, (Ger.) *Schalotte*, (It.) *scalogna, scalogno,*
(Sp.) *ascalonia, chalota*
Life Span: Hardy perennial, though grown as an annual
Appearance: Shallot plants grow to 18 inches (45 cm) in height. The
leaves are hollow, like those of a bulb onion. Occasionally white or
violet flower heads are produced, which are typically onionlike in
form. The bulbs vary in shape and color depending on the strain.
Propagation: Shallots are usually grown from sets, as the better
strains of shallots don't set seed. Be sure when you buy your first
shallots that they are genuine shallots and not a variety of multiply-
ing onion. They've become much more readily available in recent
years; many mail-order catalogs now offer shallots along with their
vegetables.

To plant, break up the clusters of bulbs, rub off the loose skins,
and plant them singly 6 inches (15 cm) apart. Press them into the
soil so tops are about an inch below the surface, and firm soil over
them. Shallots will grow at low temperatures; freezing weather
doesn't damage them, and their normal annual cycle of growth
stops soon after midsummer. In many areas they may be planted as
early as February, if soil conditions permit. In other areas fall sowing,
even when winters are severe, may give better results. Experiment
for a year or two, with a planting in both spring
and fall, to see which is better in your area.
If you live where summer temperatures
are high — say 90°F (32°C) — for pro-
longed periods, plant the bulbs in
fall. They should then mature by the
following spring.
Cultural Requirements: Soil that
produces good bulb onions is
suitable. Shallots will thrive in a
wider variety of soils than onions
but won't grow well in heavy clay or
soil with poor drainage. They need
plenty of sun. While they don't need as
frequent watering as onions, don't
allow them to dry out in the early stages
of growth. When you're weeding take

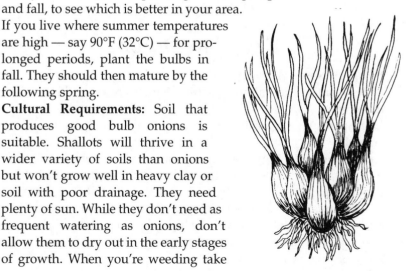

care not to damage the newly forming bulbs just under the surface. If you use mulch, keep it a few inches away from the bulbs to reduce chances of rot. When the leaves start to yellow in midsummer, draw the soil away from the little "nests" of new bulbs and withhold water to help them ripen.

Harvesting, Drying, Freezing, & Storing: When the leafy tops are turning brown, the bulbs can be lifted. If the weather is dry and sunny, leave bulbs to dry on the soil; if the weather is inclement, spread them on a wire rack under cover, so that a current of air can circulate around them. It's important not to let them get wet at this stage. Stored in net bags or nylon stockings and hung in a dry place at about 60°F (11°C), they'll keep almost indefinitely. Peel, chop, bag, and freeze them if you wish, though it's not really necessary.

Quantity to Grow: You can count on every bulb you plant producing at least eight bulbs. The first year the number you plant may have to depend on how many you can afford to buy. In later years you'll be able to use your own increase. Replant, according to your needs.

How to Use in the Kitchen: The flavor of the true shallot is distinctive and much more subtle than any others of the Allium Family. Although often considered an ingredient only of gourmet dishes, shallots can be substituted for onions in many everyday recipes. They're particularly good in dishes in which wine is used. Depending on the pungency of the shallot (different strains vary), from one to three can replace a medium-size onion. When sautéing them, never allow them to brown or they'll develop a bitter taste.

Egyptian Onions

Botanical Name: *Allium cepa*, Proliferum Group
Other Names: Top onion, topsetting winter onion, walking onion, tree onion
Life Span: A very hardy perennial, though usually grown as an annual
Appearance: The Egyptian onion has swollen stem bases from which typical onion leaves grow. An unusual member of the Allium Family, it produces tiny bulblets instead of seeds. In the second year of the plants' growth they produce a 24-inch (60-cm) stem, topped by a cluster of bulblets that look like Lilliputian onions. Green at first, then becoming reddish brown as they mature, each bulblet will grow as large as a hazelnut.

Propagation: The mature bulbs from the top of the stems are removed, separated, and planted 1 inch (2.5 cm) deep and 6 inches (15 cm) apart in the fall. This will give you scallions in early spring, long before traditional onions are ready for thinning. You can also collect bulbs in fall, store indoors over the winter, and plant in spring as early as the soil can be worked. If you don't collect the mature bulbs, their weight will cause stems to droop to the ground and they'll plant themselves (which is why they're sometimes called walking onions). The little clumps of bulblets will sprout the next year, and a year after that will produce top bulbs.

Cultural Requirements: A well-drained rich soil, as for bulb onions, and a sunny location suit these onions. Give them shelter from strong winds. Stake and tie the stems before the weight of the top onions starts to bear them down to the ground. Keep them free of weeds, and withhold water while the tiny bulbs are maturing.

Harvesting, Drying, Freezing, & Storing: The little bulblets should be harvested in early fall, when they've turned a coppery color. Dry in the sun and store in a dry, cool, frost-free place, and they'll keep well all winter. They can be frozen whole, though it isn't really necessary, as they keep so well. If you don't use all of the dried bulblets in the kitchen, they can be replanted the next year. (If you freeze them, they can't be replanted.) Use the largest bulblets in the kitchen, as they're easiest to peel; save the smallest for replanting.

Quantity to Grow: Ten bulblets, after two years' growth, will give you from 100 to 200 to eat or replant. Calculate your needs and plant accordingly.

How to Use in the Kitchen: The flavor of the underground bulbs is strong; they can be used like ordinary onions but more sparingly. Young plants are excellent as scallions; harvest before they develop their bulblet-bearing stems, which are much tougher than the leaves. The flavor of the bulblets is somewhat spicy, and they are delicious pickled.

> ## ? Did You Know?
>
> There is another Egyptian onion of American origin called the Catawissa tree onion. It grows very vigorously and, before the top bulbs have reached their full size, some of them put up stems that produce further bulblets. Only the bulblets that don't do so should be replanted. However, the clumps of these onions may be divided and replanted to multiply them. They are exceptionally hardy perennials.

Welsh Onions

Botanical Name: *Allium fistulosum*
Other Names: Bunching onions, Japanese leek, ciboules
Life Span: Hardy perennial, withstanding temperatures below 0°F (-18°C); often grown as an annual
Appearance: Welsh onions form tightly bunched, long white scallions with hollow leaves and can grow to a height of 12 to 14 inches (30–35 cm). The flowers are yellowish white pom-poms on stalks that rise above the leaves. The scallions resemble green or salad onions, except that they never form large bulbs. Natives of Siberia, they are evergreen in all but the most severe winters.
Propagation: Plant seeds in early spring or late summer; germination takes about two weeks. The tenderest spring greens and scallions come from seeds sown late the previous summer. Sow seeds 2 to 3 inches (5–7 cm) apart and ½ inch deep. Divide two- or three-year-old plants in spring or early summer. Mature plants should stand 10 inches (25 cm) apart. Small clumps can be grown in 6-inch (15-cm) pots or in a window box. Scallions may be transplanted at any size; trim any extra-long roots to make replanting easier.

Cultural Requirements: Give Welsh onions soil that's moderately fertile and well drained. Soil suitable for onions is good, though it doesn't need to be quite as rich. Choose a sheltered, well-drained, sunny spot if you want winter greens; give them some shade where summer temperatures are high. They need little care beyond routine weeding and watering. They're resistant to most onion pests and diseases, so try them if you've had trouble growing other onions.

? Did You Know?

The name *Welsh* comes from *Walisch*, meaning "foreign." These onions supposedly were introduced into England in 1624.

Harvesting, Drying, Freezing, & Storing: The green leaves can be cut from early spring to early winter in most climates. Clumps of scallions can be dug at any time of year that the ground isn't frozen. The green leaves dry well and the scallions freeze, but unless your winter is particularly severe, it's hardly worth the trouble of doing so.

Quantity to Grow: A packet of seeds (about 5 g) will sow about 40 feet of row. This should give you plenty of seedlings to supply green leaves the first year, and leave you scallions to form clumps the following year. If you're starting with plants (clumps of scallions), buy two. Within two years they'll be big enough to divide into three or four new clumps.

How to Use in the Kitchen: The flavor of the leaves is a little like chives though somewhat stronger. When chives aren't available, Welsh onions can be used as a substitute, though they're somewhat more assertive in taste. The white scallions can be used the same way you'd use "green" onion scallions. Slice them into salads or use as a garnish.

Common Pests and Diseases

The number of pests and diseases may sound formidable, but remember that you're unlikely to encounter all of them in your garden. Possibly you won't see any of them.

A few tricks will prevent or at least minimize pest and disease problems. For the most trouble-free onions, follow all of these recommendations.

1. Practice crop rotation. Move onions to a different spot in the garden each year, and don't replant onions in the same place for three to four years. Rotating is more of a challenge for perennial types of onions, but fortunately many of these (such as chives) are generally pest-resistant. If you see pests or diseases on your perennial onions, you'll need to move them each year.
2. Plant (and replant) only healthy-looking bulbs. Discard any that appear to be diseased or damaged.
3. Keep the soil well stocked with organic matter. (Compost is best.) Organic matter improves soil drainage and supplies micronutrients that increase overall plant health. In some cases, compost may provide microorganisms that suppress disease organisms.
4. Try planting ordinary onions from sets instead of seeds or transplants. Sets are more resistant to onion diseases.
5. If you've had trouble with diseases, try growing onions in raised beds, which will provide better drainage. (Be warned that because raised beds dry out more quickly, you may have to water more frequently during dry spells.) Try to site the beds in an area with good air circulation.

Insect Pests

ONION MAGGOTS. These pests are small, dirty-white larvae about ⅓ inch (1 cm) long. They hatch from eggs laid by the onion fly, which looks like a small (⅓-inch) version of the common housefly. Onion maggots may attack both bulb onions and bunching onions. When plants are infested, the leaves turn yellow and wilt. Seedlings may be destroyed, and bulbs may rot or become misshapen (they will probably contain obvious maggots when lifted). The holes left by tunneling maggots may invite diseases.

To control:
1. Pull up and destroy any infested plants as soon as you see damage.
2. Dig up all plants at the end of the season, being careful to destroy any maggots you see in the soil. If you see small brown capsules the size of wheat kernels, these are pupae and should be removed along with the plants.
3. As soon as you plant or transplant onions into the garden, cover crops with floating row covers. Support the fabric on hoops to keep it above the foliage, and secure the edges by covering with soil so no adult flies can sneak through. Floating row covers prevent onion maggot infestations by preventing adult flies from laying eggs on the plants.
4. Scattering onion sets or transplants throughout the garden may reduce damage by making it harder for adult flies to find the onions.

THRIPS. Tiny black, brown, or yellow insects, barely visible to the eye, are thrips. These pests suck sap from the leaves and cause leaves to wilt. It's easier to see the damage than the pests; look for pale or silvery blotches on the leaves and deformed plants. The damage usually shows up during hot, dry spells in July or August. In severe infestations (more common in the South than in the North), some plants may die.

To control:
1. Spray affected plants with insecticidal soap or a pyrethrin insecticide.
2. Remove and destroy any severely infested plants to improve the odds for remaining plants.
3. To help keep thrips at bay, keep your garden well weeded. Give the garden a good cleanup at the end of the season to remove the weeds in which thrips overwinter.

Diseases

BULB OR NECK ROT. This soilborne disease may affect all kinds of bulb onions. Starting in the neck, the tissues rot and become water-soaked and gray. A gray mold develops on the surface, followed by a black crust made up of little hard, black bodies. The bulbs usually become affected during the curing and storage stages.

To control:
1. The best way to control this disease is prevention. Rotating onions to a new part of the garden, and not replanting onions in the same area for at least four years, is essential for controlling this disease.
2. If your soil isn't well drained, try planting onions in raised beds. Also incorporate lots of organic matter to improve soil drainage.
3. Sow early-maturing tight-necked varieties, which are more resistant. Check catalog descriptions or ask your local Cooperative Extension Service or garden center for a good tight-necked early variety for your area.
4. Stop watering as soon as the bulbs start to ripen.
5. Lift, dry, and store bulbs as recommended (see pages 10–12).

DOWNY MILDEW. This is a fungus disease that overwinters in the bulbs or in the soil. In the spring, it causes yellow spots to appear on the leaves as they start to grow, and later a fuzzy purplish mildew will cover these spots. The disease will check the growth of the bulbs and infect the soil. It usually appears where conditions are very damp, or after a month of damp, cool weather.

To control:
1. Remove any leaves with yellow spots as soon as you see them. This may slow or stop the disease if the weather improves.
2. Cultivate the soil only when it is dry.
3. Once you've seen downy mildew in your garden, plant onions in a location away from any onion relatives that have overwintered and are still in the ground. If your soil is infected, don't replant with onion relatives for three or four years.
4. If the soil isn't well drained, mix in lots of organic matter. Try growing onions and onion relatives in raised beds for improved drainage.

PINK ROOT ROT. This disease is more common on bulb onions and scallions; leeks and chives are less susceptible and Welsh onions (the species, not necessarily hybrids) are immune. The main symptom is plants that appear to be stunted. To check for the disease, pull up a plant. If plants are infected, some roots will have rotted and remaining roots will be pink, not the usual white.

To control:
1. Pull up and destroy any infected plants. Don't toss them on the compost pile (it may not get hot enough to kill the disease) — toss them out!
2. As this disease may get a foothold through wounds, it's important to avoid injuring the bulbs during cultivation. Control onion maggots (see page 28), as their tunnels also give this disease a foothold.
3. If the soil isn't well drained, mix in lots of organic matter. Try growing onions and onion relatives in raised beds for improved drainage.
4. Seek out varieties that show some tolerance to pink root; if you can't find this information in catalog descriptions, ask your local Cooperative Extension Service. Tolerance (unlike resistance) doesn't mean your onions won't get the disease, but it does mean you have a better chance of getting a decent harvest.
5. Once you've seen pink root, follow an eight-year crop rotation. Pink root is caused by a fungus that can survive in the soil for at least six years, so if you plant onions in the same spot within that time, you're asking for trouble. Plant onions in a location away from any onion relatives that have overwintered and are still in the ground. Wait eight years before replanting onions in once-infected soil.

ONION SMUT. This disease attacks onions, leeks, shallots, and chives. It causes brownish, elongated, blisterlike markings to appear on the young leaves of seedling plants. Eventually, a swelling or hardened area develops just above the neck; if this bursts, it will release a black powder (reproductive spores) that will spread the disease.

To control:
1. Pull up and destroy any infected plants. Don't toss them on the compost pile (it may not get hot enough to kill the disease) — toss them out!
2. If the soil isn't well drained, mix in lots of organic matter. Try growing onions and onion relatives in raised beds for improved drainage.
3. Practice a three- to four-year crop rotation.

Suppliers

Fedco Co-op Garden Supplies
207-873-7333
www.fedcoseeds.com

Gurney's Seed & Nursery Co.
513-354-1491
www.gurneys.com

Johnny's Selected Seeds
877-564-6697
www.johnnyseeds.com

Main Street Seed & Supply Company
866-229-3276
www.mainstreetseedandsupply.com

Victory Heirloom Seeds
info@victoryseeds.com
www.victoryseeds.com